FROM SAD TO GLAD:

HELPING YOUR DOG SURVIVE A LOSS

by

Phoebe Lauren, J.D.

ISBN-13: 978-1530359097
Copyright © 2016 by Phoebe Lauren
All rights reserved

*A dog will teach you unconditional love.
If you can have that in your life,
things won't be too bad.*

> Robert Wagner

INTRODUCTION

Many books have been written about how we grieve when our pets die or are lost, but little has been written about how our pets grieve. While I believe that pets and animals of all kinds have the capacity to grieve, this book focuses mainly on dogs, one of the most widely owned pets in the Western world. You can probably guess what the other popular pet is. Meow!!

When a pet dies, we may spend a lot of time feeling sad and even lonely; but we rarely consider the other animals in the household. Remember when we go through big changes, our dogs, like us, are creatures of habit and they can be highly emotional and subject to insecurities. Dogs miss their playmates as much as we do. When a dog's owner dies, it can be a devastating event. They may grieve for days, months, or years and no one may notice!

Of course behind every book there is usually a story. This is mine. The first time I became aware of a dog feeling sadness was with the death of my son, Marcus, who had a life-threatening disease.

We had a dog, named Hopi, who was his faithful companion from age four until his death at age ten. The two of them were extremely bonded and went everywhere together. Marcus died at home in his own bed. Hopi went outside his room and howled. Her heart was broken. Now, no one can tell me that dogs do not grieve or that they don't realize when something awful happens. Of course they do.

At Marcus's memorial service Hopi howled when a friend played the violin. It must have reminded her of Marcus since that was the instrument he had played. Sadly, at the time I wasn't able to help Hopi. I had my hands full, doing everything I could to survive, finish law school, and keep my marriage together.

Frankly, I didn't even notice that Hopi was grieving because my own loss was so great. Just recently I asked Marcus's father where Hopi was after Marcus's death. He told me he took care of her while we were still together. I have no memory of even having a dog. He told me she grieved for about four years. We were divorced by the time Hopi recovered! She was such a sweet dog who slowly limped along until her death. Looking back on this situation, I now know that when Hopi died it was of a broken heart. Her sadness and my inability to recognize that she needed help have motivated me to write this book.

While I am not a veterinarian or a pet therapist, I have spent a lot of time around dogs and have researched how animals grieve. More importantly, I have the capacity to *listen* to animals and hear what they are telling us. While I don't refer to myself as an animal communicator, I think of myself more as a sensitive *listener* to animals. You will be surprised what you can learn simply by observing and listening to your own pet. I was also an attorney some years ago and maybe that gives me the ability or experience to ask animals the right questions! I want to share with you what I have learned along with some of the best information available.

When you finish reading this book, you too will be able to recognize the signs of grief in your dog and to remedy them or to know when you might need to seek expert help. While this is a book *for* dogs, since they can't read (or at least we don't think they can), I am writing this for dog owners everywhere!

So let's get started!

I have found that when you are deeply troubled, there are things you get from the silent devoted companionship of a dog that you can get from no other source.

Doris Day

WHAT DO DOGS GRIEVE?

Many people don't realize it, but pets grieve separation and changing situations just like we do. These may be brought on by anything, including death of their owner, separation through divorce, change of residence, a teenager going off to college, and of course the loss of their own pet companions, be they of the same species or not. A dog may be extremely close to another dog, a cat, a bird, or any other animal.

The beginning of strong inter-species bonding between humans and dogs dates back thousands of years. Today, after all this time, there is a strong bonding between dogs and humans – they are, in other words, finely tuned into us. They recognize our joy and our sadness. Haven't you ever noticed the attention a dog will give you when you are sick or sad? Sometimes, they will even cry with us.

Of course, there is the discussion as to whether a dog actually grieves or is merely picking up our sadness. My question is this: Does it really matter? If a dog is sad and exhibiting the signs of grief, then it is grieving!

The amount of grieving your animal experiences is directly dependent on his or her relationship with what has been lost. And of course, dogs are as unique as people and each grieves in his or her own way. If the dog is devoted to one person in the family and that person is missing for whatever reason, your pet may grieve.

I remember once when I had a very bad cold/flu and could hardly breathe. I was staying with a friend who had a dog, which always slept in his room by his bed at night. However, when I was really sick, his dog stayed all night long by my side in a bedroom down the hallway. She didn't leave my side until I was much better. At that point, she simply returned to my friend's bedroom, never to sleep near me again. I often wonder if her job was to heal me, but that's another whole subject. Clearly, she was picking up something since she was a very finely tuned being – this is a small example of the kind of sensitive interaction that can take place between one dog and one person.

Because dogs have distinct personalities, some will grieve much harder and much longer than others. It depends on the sensitivity of the animal. Some pets are completely bonded with their owners and move as if they were one with them. Everywhere the owner goes, the dog is by his or her side. Others are more carefree and distance themselves.

Just as each dog is unique, so is the grieving process. This is exactly the same with people. How much we grieve depends largely on what kind of relationship we had with the person, animal, or thing that we have lost. Grieving also depends on our experiences in life. This is true for dogs as well.

Here are some examples:

One of our dogs is a rescue dog. Her name is Lily and we found her in a shelter. She had been adopted out two times by two different families, only to be returned when she "didn't work out". When we found Lily she was practically furless, very small, lethargic and pretty scared. On her record, it was reported that she had issues with big black dogs. Of course, at the time we had a Bernese mountain dog – black and tan. The first night, Lily attacked our other dog. Then we had an idea to separate them at feeding time. From that point on there was no longer a problem although Lily did try to run away a few times.

By the way, Lily had been treated by a dog therapist who found her very insecure. No one thought that Lily attacked the bigger dogs in the family simply because she was hungry. So much for psychology – sometimes simple reasoning and observation work best!

Lily has bonded somewhat with humans and other dogs, but rolls rather easily with the punches. She's has been separated from me and her dog companions without showing signs of grieving. The first time, she lost her good friend, Katy, the Bernese, by death and more recently she experienced separation from her new friend, Charlie, a Lab, who had been off at training school. The thing that is so special about Lily is that she likes everyone, generally is happy, and seems very secure, just as long as her environment stays the same.

Lily lived out in the country in the high desert for three years and when that house was sold, she started acting out almost immediately by staying close to her owners, peeing in the house, and dragging her little bed cushion out into the hallway from the bedroom. Obviously, she sensed the upcoming move and was afraid she'd be left behind. Because she had been traumatized by having been returned to the shelter two times, she acts out each time there is a potential move. This is her way of "saying" she doesn't want things to change and she doesn't want to go anywhere else. Although she always appears happy-go-lucky, underneath it all is a scared little darling – one who grieves any change of residence with an enormous fear that those she loves will go away and leave her or take her back to that cage at the shelter.

Here's another example:

Jon Tumilson's dog, Hawkeye, was an important part of his life and Jon was also very important to Hawkeye. Jon was a Navy Seal and was killed one summer in Afghanistan. Many friends and family attended his funeral in Iowa "including his 'son' Hawkeye, a black Labrador retriever who, with a heavy sigh, lay down in front of Tumilson's flag-draped casket. There the loyal dog stayed for the entire service." Maryann Mott, *HealthDay News*.

While Hawkeye created a lot of buzz in the media, he is just one of many dogs who has grieved his owner's death.

Another very touching story: There was the case of Wiley the wolf dog who was so fond of his owner's late grandmother, Gladys, that he appeared to cry at her graveside. The adorable wolf dog lay on the tombstone and seemed to be distraught at the loss, shaking, and making what appeared to be sobbing noises as the family gathered around him. James Gordon, *Daily Mail* online.

I wanted to give you some examples so that you, the reader, will know that not all dogs grieve and certainly not all dogs grieve in the same way. Transitions are difficult enough for us, but at least we can use our reasoning to muddle through. Dogs obviously don't have that possibility. Let's look more closely at what dogs grieve, so that you will be aware of the types of circumstances that may trigger grief.

1. Loss of a person in the family, be it through death, divorce, illness, travel, work, or any other reason. It doesn't matter to your dog why a person he has bonded to is gone. As far as your dog is concerned the person is gone, and your dog doesn't know if that person will ever come back.

2. Loss of another household pet – whether of the same species or not through death, loss, or rehoming.

3. Change of residence – dogs like the familiar, it makes them feel safe.

4. Loss of an activity – for instance, a show dog who is too old and is no longer the center of attention; or when a child leaves for college and isn't there to play ball everyday; or a master who is incapable of going for walks for whatever reason.

5. Loss of being the only dog – most dogs love being the center of attention and may be jealous or resentful of a new pet being added to the family.

6. Loss of the center of attention by the addition of a baby, which will certainly make him feel displaced. He may wonder why all the "oohs" and "aahs" are suddenly no longer focused on him, especially if he's used to being an only dog.

7. Any change of routine, especially if the person who has always been home is suddenly gone – perhaps off to work during the day.

8. Any addition to the family, such as a new spouse and/or stepchildren may cause your pet to grieve. Suppose you were a single man or woman – it was just you and faithful Fido when along comes the love of your life, accompanied by four new kids, a bird, and two cats. Well, who wouldn't grieve?

So, in conclusion, every time there is a transition in your life, remember it is also happening to your dog. Dr. Christopher Pachel, a Board Certified Veterinary Behaviorist, agrees with me: *"A dog that experiences any kind of major change, such as the introduction of a new child or a move of residence, can show signs of depression."*

Dogs are like sponges, they pick up on your every emotion. If you are feeling harried, fearful, depressed, sick, and tired, you can be sure your dog companion is also picking up on these feelings. The only difference is that your dog doesn't know what's happening to cause these upsets. If you can, try putting yourself in your dog's place. Imagine what she's seeing during a change of residence – stuff being shifted around, people all over the house touching her things and she doesn't know that you "we" are moving. She has no idea of the future – all she sees is what's in front of her nose. Her little eyes are looking right and then left – her whole world is being turned upside down, but she doesn't know why. Of course, she's confused and may be sad or anxious.

Anytime there is a change, please do observe your dog and give him a few extra reassuring pats. Any kind of change is stressful, even so called good ones. For instance you may be moving to a larger house, maybe your dream house. However, your dog isn't aware of what's happening during a change of residence; and if he suddenly finds himself in a new environment, he doesn't know where his place is and that's scary even for the biggest and bravest dog!

So let's see what a dog does when grieving. In the next chapter, we'll look at possible symptoms.

SIGNS YOUR PET IS GRIEVING

"Dogs are wise. They crawl away into a quiet corner and lick their wounds and do not rejoin the world until they are whole once more." Agatha Christy, a mystery writer.

While this is true for some dogs and of course, I do believe most dogs are wiser than we are, remember no two are alike and each one will have a different response to loss and change. *"Some may show signs of physical sadness, while others may display symptoms of negative behavior, and some may not show any sign of emotional suffering at all."* Cesar Millan, a self trained dog behaviorist, known for his show, the Dog Whisperer.

So let's consider signs of sadness first, which you may or may not recognize. A depressed dog is rather like a depressed person. The dog may walk around with his head down, drooping along with little energy like Hopi. She may sleep a lot more than usual and change her eating habits by either eating more or less than usual. She may also drink a lot less as if she no longer wants to live. He may not feel like playing with his toys and just be generally sluggish. Often, a dog will withdraw from everyone, stop barking, and stay in a corner or hidden under the bed. She may also suddenly turn clingy and not want to be apart from the rest of the family, when before the loss, she was very independent. In other words, a dog may lose interest in life, even to the point of not wanting to go for walks.

You may find your dog wandering around the house as if searching for the person or pet that is no longer there. He may go to places where he spent time with his friend. He may even let out a howl from time to time. He may also spend endless hours looking out the window hoping his playmate or owner will come back home. This is especially true if your other dog went away still alive, as when it is euthanized or it dies in an accident away from home. If a member of the family leaves and doesn't return, the dog may wait endless days and continue to search for the missing person or playmate. Remember your dog may mourn any other household animal he was close to, whether a dog or not.

Dogs may also begin to lick their paws incessantly, which can be a reaction to stress, due to an emotional problem such as grief or anxiety. I've heard of dogs licking their paws raw after a loss. Some dogs lose some or all of their fur after a great shock. If this is happening to your dog, take him to the vet to rule out skin allergies or other physical problems before assuming an emotional issue is the culprit.

These symptoms may come on all at once lasting only a short time, or they may come on gradually and can last months or even years. It's important to be observant, especially since you may also be feeling sad from the loss or change. We must be vigilant since we don't really know what our dog is thinking, after all he can't tell us. So we can only observe his behavior and actions and interpret them as best we can.

Now let's look at negative behavior which is something more easily recognized. A dog who is house broken may start to do his business in the house, on your rugs, or anywhere where he never peed or pooped before. She may start chewing on everything in sight, destroying things she never touched before. Your dog may even show his teeth, growl, or snap and become aggressive. You will wonder whatever happened to your nice well-behaved dog. Think no further, your dog is in mourning and striking out at anything and anyone in order to express his unhappiness. This kind of negative behavior is a sure sign of grieving.

Dogs are very sensitive to the feelings of their owners and to the general atmosphere in the household. They often take on your feelings, so if you're depressed they will be too. Some dogs will go into a tizzy if you start to cry – they may try to jump up on you or even start to howl. Your pain is their pain. I believe that dogs help us grieve and get over our losses, but this is just my idea. On the other hand, I know a dog that withdrew completely from his owner, as if the owner's grief and pain were too much to bear.

If you find your dog howling or barking more than usual, it is important to try to distract him, but never reward negative behavior. If your dog does something "bad", distraction and not yelling are the best solutions. Do not give him a treat, as that will reinforce the negative behavior.

Remember to reinforce what you like your dog to do and not what you don't want!

So after a loss or a major change in your life, do be on the look out for changes in your dog's behavior. It's important because you can then help your dog through his grief and in doing so, it will help you heal as well.

GRIEVING ANIMALS IN GENERAL

Now I'm not saying that dogs are the only animals that grieve, and I'm sure many of you have seen videos of animals in mourning on YouTube. There's one of Tara, the elephant, mourning the loss of her companion Bella, a dog that was probably killed by coyotes. And then there's the mother dolphin, seen carrying a dead baby calf for days in the China Sea. Koka, the gorilla, communicated through sign language that she was sad when she was told that her pet kitten had been hit by a car and died. And especially touching is a video of penguins mourning the death of a tiny emperor penguin chick.

So while it's true that many animal species mourn, I've chosen to concentrate on dogs simply because we live with them on a daily basis and can do so much to help them. For those of you who are interested in other species and how they grieve, please have a look at *How Animals Grieve,* a book by Barbara King, Chancellor Professor of Anthropology at William & Mary.

A story that is very close to my heart concerns a horse that was in mourning in Holland. It was the first time that I had ever worked with a horse and a sad one at that. She had been flown over from Australia and was in a new stable, a very nice one out in the countryside. After listening to her, I realized that she didn't know where she was and where her previous owner was. She was in deep mourning and had a lot of confusion over the changes in her surroundings.

I asked the new owner what had happened. He explained that she had been anesthetized and had been flown over to Holland. Once I heard this, I was able to explain to the horse that her previous owner was in Australia and that while she was very much loved she was now in a new place which was also very nice. She immediately calmed down and felt better, but not before she asked me to clean out her stall because she didn't like the energy of the last horse that had been in it. I did that through prayer. We communicated for a long time, and she seemed grateful that someone could finally explain the situation to her.

Really, I had no idea if I'd been of any help or not. Later that day, I was outside with the owner and a few friends drinking tea, when I heard a horse whinnying. I look up and there she was with her head held high. The owner smiled and said it was the first time since she'd arrived that her head wasn't drooping. She looked quite happy and I was thrilled to have been a part of her healing.

And for those of you who haven't seen the movie, *A Dog's Tale* starring Richard Gere, it's a must. It's based on the true story of a dog named Hachiko who waited for his master at the same place every day after his death for ten years. Hachiko would go to the train station and sit until his master's train came in and then, not finding him there, he would go home until the next day. Such a beautiful story of love and devotion and it certainly takes away all doubt that dogs grieve. In a way, dogs are lucky because they don't seem to realize the finality of death. They have the option of hoping that their loved one might come back.

It seems that many animals grieve in much the same way that we do. This research and documentation is pretty recent, thanks to modern technology. More and more caretakers are becoming sensitive to this issue and are helping our animal friends overcome their losses. Please feel free to use the tips in this book with whatever animal you may be working with as you see fit.

The greatest fear dogs know is the fear that you will not come back when you go out the door without them.

Stanley Coren

HELPING YOUR DOG SURVIVE LOSS AND CHANGE

Ask yourself what is it you want or need most when you are feeling sad, and you will quickly have an idea of many things that you can do to comfort your dog. Two of the cardinal rules are these:

1. Attempt to maintain a normal routine as much as humanly possible as far as the essentials go, like feeding and walking times and where your dog sleeps.

2. Pay as much attention as possible to your dog.

At first, these rules may seem simple and they are, unless you are grieving as well, which is often the case. That's why I cannot impress enough upon you how necessary and important these two things are. If you are grieving, you may totally forget to feed your dog or take him for a walk. This is normal and to be expected. One thing that can be helpful is to set a reminder on your cell phone. Don't just have your phone ring, but write down what you are supposed to do. "Feed Fido!"

It may seem like a ridiculous idea if you've never experienced deep sadness or grief, but believe me it can be a lifesaver.

Routine is a comfort to your dog and it will also help you get through trying days. Dogs, like most people, need to have the least amount of disruption of everyday activities when they are coping with change. It's very important that you continue to feed your dog the same brand of food at the same times every day, with maybe a few treats thrown in here and there. We'll get to that in a few minutes.

As far as sleeping goes, your dog needs his bedding – remember familiarity breeds contentment. If you are in the middle of a move, be sure to pull out his bedding, whether it is a cushion or a dog bed. Don't put it in the moving truck, but take it with you if at all possible. That way when you arrive at your destination it's there; and if you have to stay a night or two in a hotel enroute, your dog can sleep more peacefully. Also, your dog may feel safer in an enclosed space in an unfamiliar environment, so you might want to provide a kennel for him or her (just leave it in a room with a few of his toys in it and the door open).

Remember the idea of a doggie bag when moving, but in this case it can be a doggie box. In it put his blanket, his feeding bowls, and some of his favorite toys. This box should be unpacked early on if not first thing. So even though your dog may be grieving his old digs, he will begin to feel right at home when he is surrounded by his familiar things. If you have a rug that he likes to lie on, why not put that down as soon as possible? There's nothing like an old rug in the den to create a cozy safe atmosphere for him. And if he follows you from room to room, praise him. Tell him what each room is – "this is the bedroom, this is the kitchen" – that way he will start to learn the layout of his new home.

Once your dog's basic needs are met, there are plenty of other things you can do to help her heal. Giving your dog extra attention is very important and can certainly be comforting for you as well. Just five minutes everyday can make a world of difference. Here are some ideas:

1. Give your dog little food treats – such as his favorite canned food or doggie treats from time to time. Remember not to change his diet in a radical way; however, little occasional treats can be reassuring and provide a bit of pleasure. This is especially useful if your dog refuses to eat his normal food or if he is eating much less than usual. If your dog is sad because you've added a puppy to the family who gets to eat two or three times a day, be sure to give your first dog a little treat while the puppy is eating.

Speaking of treats, although you may crave chocolate like I do under these circumstances, do not give it to your dog as chocolate can kill him.

2. If you have added a dog to your family, your only dog may feel displaced, so it's important to give your first dog plenty of attention. The first dog should still get attention first, meals first, greeted first, and fussed over first – at least until she adjusts to the new addition. If you have bonded closely with your first dog, remember to take her out on walks and outings alone sometimes, so she can still feel special. Once your first dog realizes she is still very important, you can start giving equal attention to both without hurting her feelings.

3. Create rituals that your dog can look forward to. If your dog likes to be brushed or massaged, do offer that to her perhaps after dinner every few days. This is a way to tell your dog that you love and care about her. Some dogs feel special going to a dog groomer and coming back all clean and fresh smelling, yet another treat!

4. Sometimes all your dog needs to make him feel better is just a pat on the head and a few well chosen words spoken in a gentle way. Remember your dog is recovering from a trauma so being gentle with him is restorative. Let him know that you know this is a tough time – talk to your dog even if you aren't sure how much he understands.

5. Allow your dog to stay in the room of the person who has gone. If this isn't possible, provide a piece of clothing with the scent of that person. If your dog has lost his dog companion, keeping an old blanket or another article with the scent of the deceased dog can be a comfort. The remaining dog will like to have familiar scents around, enabling him to say good-bye eventually. Remember dogs have an incredible sense of smell.

6. Playing games with your dog always helps. Keep your dog busy by hiding toys or treats in her favorite spots to find throughout the day. A good place is in her kennel. She will be surprised and enjoy the treat even more. You can hide in the house with doggie treats in your pocket. Believe me, your dog will find you!

7. Invite over friends who have dogs that your dog likes, especially if she has lost her dog companion. You may also arrange a play date for your dog with another one. Dogs, like humans, have favorite human friends so invite them over too.

8. And finally, provide as much pleasure as possible. If your dog loved to play ball before her loss, she may love playing fetch with you now. If she had a special place to walk like along a creek or in a dog park, take her there as often as you can. Some dogs enjoy a certain kind of music, or a dip in a pond, or even a TV show. Whatever your dog's favorite activities are, do try to provide them

frequently, as one day soon she will begin to smile again and jump for joy.

Now that we've looked at the positive side, let's consider what you can do if your dog is exhibiting less than desirable behavior. As long as your dog isn't a real danger to anyone, you should consider unwanted behavior as a passing phase.

If your dog is doing his business in the house, try taking him for more frequent walks. Pay attention and make sure he is actually relieving himself. If that doesn't help, then confine him to one room or area of the house until the behavior improves. It will do no good to yell at your dog as he already feels bad enough, and it will simply add to his stress and could cause him to have more accidents.

If your dog is acting out by chewing on everything in sight, try to give him something appropriate to chew on like a big bone toy from the pet store. There are so many toys now that can be chewed on and not destroyed, at least not immediately. If your dog is acting out by chewing, be sure to put valuables where he can't reach them. If he's chewing on furniture, etc., then try to keep an eye on him. If you leave, put him in his kennel or in a confined space until you can trust him again. This, too, is usually a passing behavior and as your dog becomes more secure he will normally stop.

Now if your dog is showing aggressive behavior, this is an entirely different matter. You must take action to protect others and to protect your other animals. A dog that has always tolerated the house cat may not be so kind when he himself is hurting. So try to keep your animals safe and separated if necessary. If your dog is not used to children, then it's a good idea to put him in another room should children come to visit. And if you have a small dog and the one that is grieving is alpha dog, be on the lookout for aggressive acts. All in all a little bit of prevention is worth it. Think ahead as much as possible. If your dog is feeling snarly, isolate him as much as needed.

Remember dogs are pack animals. Whether it's the leader dog that leaves or the follower dog, your dog's position in the pack has changed. You may now have a former leader dog without a follower or a former follower dog without a canine leader. If the alpha dog dies, the other dog may have less confidence and be more fearful and withdrawn without the other's protection. This is just something to notice and then you can reassure the timid dog that she is still safe. If she doesn't feel like walking outside past other dogs where she once felt protected by the leader, try taking her on a walk following a different route. It's also possible that under the same circumstances, the less dominant dog may suddenly blossom because she is no longer dependent on the leader.

Dogs are our link to paradise. They don't know evil or jealousy or discontent. To sit with a dog on a hillside on a glorious afternoon is to be back in Eden, where doing nothing was not boring --it was peace.

Milan Kundera

WHEN TO SEEK OUTSIDE HELP

Let's say that you have tried everything in this book and others and your dog is still feeling sad and withdrawn or exhibiting other signs of depression. It's a good idea to have him looked at by a veterinarian. Dogs, just like people, often develop illnesses after a change or loss. The first year after such a shock many people become ill and so do their pets. So, if you feel that the grieving is wearing your dog down, do take him to the vet.

Of course, if you find yourself unable to take care of your dog or to do the simplest tasks because of the grief you are feeling, please take action. There are so many good books that you can read about overcoming your own loss. Ask around and try to find a sharing group that helps people deal with grief. Your best resources may be your church, the library, or a nearby hospital. Almost every city now has grief counselors as well. If you are too harassed and stressed out to deal with your dog's problems, they may grow in size. Your dog picks up your feelings and he may become confused and feel neglected and eventually fall ill.

Remember some dogs experience sadness right away and others take time, but if your dog has seemed rather normal after a change and then suddenly becomes very lethargic, a vet visit is a good idea. One thing your vet may suggest is drug therapy to help reduce your dog's anxiety and to help him cope better.

Once physical illness is ruled out, then you might also want to consider contacting a pet therapist or communicator. The only advice I have here is to try to find someone whom your vet recommends. If that's not possible, I would turn to my friends and attempt to get a referral from one of them, because there are many people who claim to be pet therapists who are really interested only in your money. As far as I know, there are no necessary trainings to become a pet therapist, so remember to use your intelligence when dealing with one.

Just to reassure you that your dog is okay and will heal, I want to tell you what the American Society for the Prevention of Cruelty to Animals found out when they conducted a Companion Animal Mourning Project. "The study found that 36% of dogs ate less than usual after the death of another canine companion. About 11% actually stopped eating completely. About 63% of dogs vocalized more than normal or became quieter. Study respondents indicated that surviving dogs changed the quantity and location of sleep. More than half the surviving pets became more affectionate and clingy with their caregivers. Overall, the study revealed that 66% of dogs exhibited four or more behavioral changes after losing a pet companion." PetPlace.com Staff

So your dog is not alone. The only thing I would add is that loss of any kind can and does produce the types of changes this study found. Furthermore, if a dog is closely bonded to a person, I can imagine that these symptoms of grieving will be even more pronounced.

Some people have wondered how long a dog might grieve. The answer to that is not simple. Dogs take however long they need to recuperate, just like we humans do. Pet experts believe it may take anywhere from a few week to as long as six months before a dog begins to feel like his old self again. Remember though in Hopi's case, she grieved for years. So don't expect a quick fix, yet there are so many actions you can take to help your pet during this recovery period.

Try to keep your dog busy doing things she loves – fun activities. Those activities depend on what your dog likes to do, what she enjoys. For some, it's walking and for others it might be playing fetch, or being with other dogs or with children. Each dog is as unique as we are. Of course, this goes without saying because if you've had several dog friends you already know this.

MOVING ON

Most dog owners can feel and observe when their dog is ready to move on. You will find your old pal has returned, that his tail is wagging more frequently and that the blues seem to have disappeared. Once again he is jumping on your bed in the morning ready to go for an early walk. He's eating and sleeping again as he did before.

When most of the signs of mourning are over, your dog is ready and wants to resume life as usual. Of course, she will still like to have all the attention you can give her, but she'll also be ready to put her little winter coat on and head out to play in the snow or in the warmer climates, she'll be ready to go play at the beach.

To help you and your dog resume normal life, begin by trying to vary routine once again. It won't be so important to him to eat at the same time everyday or go for walks punctually, although remember dogs do love routine. I know one dog that stands next to his feeding bowl everyday at noon, lest his owner forget to feed him!

When your dog feels better, it's important for you to attempt to put on a happy face as well – to be cheerful even if it may take you a bit longer to recover from the loss. When you invest time in your dog's healing you will be paid back in so many ways. The companionship of your dog can help you muddle through because his needs will make you feel needed and take your mind off your own problems. If your dog loves outings, then get your walking shoes out and go to the dog park or beach. Some dogs simply love the movement of being in the car, so move, move, move.

Now if you have had one of your dogs die or go away, you may think it's healing to get another one right away. Everything that I've read says it's a good idea to wait a while, some say as long as a year. I believe that you will know when you, other family members, and your remaining dog(s) are ready to welcome a new pet into the household. The one thing I wouldn't recommend is to rush out and find a substitute dog. Give everyone in your family time to heal, including your remaining dog or dogs. Everyone grieves differently and if someone in the family is taking the loss very hard, then it's best to wait and not force a new dog into your home.

Remember that a newcomer will add stress to your dog's life. Your dog will have to adjust once again to yet another change. Also, don't forget that some dogs love being an *only* dog, so it's certainly not always necessary to get a companion dog. If you do decide to get another dog, wait until your present dog's negative behavior has stopped; otherwise, the new dog may think it perfectly natural to pee in the house and bark constantly! Even if you've had two dogs of the same sex before, consider getting a dog of the opposite sex, as it will reduce friction between them.

This advice goes especially if you have lost your only dog. Give yourself time to adjust before getting another dog companion. If not, you may find yourself in the uncomfortable position of comparing the new dog to your old one. The dance that takes place between a human being and his dog is magical and mysterious. Just like any relationship, it takes time to grow and to flow.

Finally, please remember to pay attention to your pets whether they are grieving or not, as they give us so much and expect so little in return. We sometimes treat our pets more as an object rather than a living being with their own needs and concerns. So be kind and attentive to your pet's needs. When you focus a little more on them during your times of trouble, you will find it healing for both of you.

I sincerely hope that you have found this book valuable and that the tips in it will provide comfort for your dog while he or she overcomes loss. We are so blessed to have our dog companions who give us so much unconditional love. While you, too, may be coping with loss and change, at least you will have these tools in your hands as a way to say thank you to your dog for all the kindness and caring he or she has given you.

May all your days be filled with the joy that only a dog can bring into one's life.

Heaven is the place where all the dogs you've ever loved come to meet you.

Unknown

About the author:

Phoebe Lauren is an international author, lecturer, and workshop leader. She is an ordained interfaith minister, a certified spiritual counselor, and a former attorney. Phoebe lives between Europe and the U.S.A.

She has written twenty books on a variety of subjects, available for purchase in soft cover or as eBooks on Amazon sites worldwide. Her books have been published in several languages. You can read more about her work and a short description of each book at:

http://phoebelauren.com

Printed in Great Britain
by Amazon